Stellar Science Fiction
CRAFTS

by Jen Jones

4D™

An Augmented Reading Crafting Experience

CAPSTONE PRESS
a capstone imprint

Dabble Lab Books are published by Capstone Press,
1710 Roe Crest Drive
North Mankato, Minnesota 56003

www.mycapstone.com

Library of Congress Cataloging-in-Publication Data
Cataloging-in-Publication Data is available on the Library of Congress website.
ISBN 978-1-5435-0686-0 (library binding)
ISBN 978-1-5435-0690-7 (eBook PDF)

Editorial Credits
Mari Bolte, editor; Lori Bye and Bobbie Nuytten, designers; Morgan Walters, media
researcher; Kathy McColley, production specialist

Photo Credits:
All photographs by Capstone Studio/Karon Dubke except: Shutterstock: Business
stock, design element throughout, Neti.OneLove, design element throughout

Printed and bound in the USA.
010760S18

TABLE OF CONTENTS

MORE POWER TO YOU 6

ALTERNATE TIMELINE 8

DINO STYLE 10

TOTALLY TUBULAR 12

BLAST-OFF BOT 16

GROW-BOT 18

OFFBEAT OASIS 20

SPACE CASE 22

UP AND AWAY 28

READ MORE 32

MAKERSPACE TIPS 32

INTERNET SITES 32

Anything You Can Imagine

Dinosaurs roaming the planet. Cities that float in the sky. People traveling through time and space. Aliens among us. In science-fiction (aka "sci-fi") books, anything is possible, thanks to limitless imagination and creativity. And that goes for sci-fi-inspired crafts too!

In this book, sci-fi goes DIY with projects inspired by the wonderful and wacky world of science fiction. You'll tap into a whole new world (or worlds!) of possibilities.

Download the Capstone 4D app!

- Ask an adult to search in the Apple App Store or Google Play for "Capstone 4D".
- Click Install (Android) or Get, then Install (Apple).
- Open the app.
- Scan any of the following spreads with this icon:

When you scan a spread, you'll find fun extra stuff to go with this book! You can also find these things on the web at *www.capstone4D.com* using the password: ncc.scifi

More
POWER
To You

Just like the superheroes of sci-fi, we've all got secret powers. What's yours? This adorable pennant banner poses that very question for everyday inspiration.

What You'll Need:

ruler
scissors
colored cardstock
old book pages
thin cardboard, such
    as an old cereal box
white paper
glue stick
hole punch
twine

Steps:

1. Measure and cut 20 triangles from the cardstock. The short end of the triangle should be 6 inches (15.2 centimeters) wide. The long sides should each measure 9 inches (23 cm). Set the triangles aside.

2. Measure and cut 20 triangles from the old book pages. The short side should be 5 inches (12.7 cm) wide. The long sides should be 7 inches (17.8 cm) long.

3. Set the cardboard on your workspace. Cut it into a 6-inch square. Use scissors to make scalloped cuts along the edge to make a burst shape.

4. Use the cardboard template to trace and cut out 20 bursts from the white paper.

5. Use a computer to type and print *What's Your Superpower?* in 300-point font. Cut out each letter.

6. Glue a book page triangle to the middle of a colored triangle. Add a burst, and then add a letter. The triangles should face downward.

7. Repeat step 6 until all the triangles are assembled.

8. Use a hole punch to make a hole at the top corners of the triangles. These will be your pennants.

9. Thread the pennants onto the twine. Then hang to display.

2.

3.

8.

9.

ALTERNATE TIMELINE

Ever wish you could go back in time?
This creatively themed clock is about
as close as it gets in real life.

What You'll Need:

14-inch (35.6 cm) embroidery hoop
cardboard
scissors
iron
1/2 yard (0.45 meters) fabric
craft glue
letter stencil
fabric paint and fine paintbrush
felt adhesive-back numbers

Steps:

1. Loosen the screw to separate the two pieces of the embroidery hoop.

2. Trace the outline of the smaller circle onto a piece of cardboard. Then cut it out.

3. Ask an adult to help you iron the fabric. Place the fabric on top of the smaller hoop. Reattach the larger hoop by tightening the screw.

4. Trim away any excess fabric.

5. Flip the hoop over. Glue the cardboard circle to the back of the fabric. Let the glue dry completely.

6. Arrange numbers 1–12 along the outside of the hoop. When you like how they look, remove the backing and press the numbers into place.

7. Use the stencil to lightly trace the words Back in Time onto the fabric.

8. When the letters are placed to your liking, fill them in with fabric paint. Let the paint dry completely before hanging your clock.

1.

6.

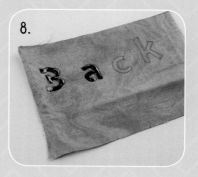

8.

NOW TRY THIS!

Give your clock a true flashback in time by arranging the numbers in reverse order! Or place them randomly to make time wobble.

DINO STYLE

Need a new tote to lug all those sci-fi books back and forth from the library? This prehistoric-inspired pouch will keep them from being lost out in the world.

What You'll Need:

old photo frame
masking tape
tracing paper
photo of a dinosaur
scissors
adhesive-back foam sheets
fabric paint and foam paintbrush
tote bag

1.

3.

Steps:

1. Take the photo frame apart. Discard the backing and the frame. Cover glass edges with masking tape to protect yourself from cuts. Set the glass aside.

2. Use the tracing paper to trace your dino photo. Then cut it out.

3. Trace and cut out the dino shape onto the foam sheet. Repeat two more times until you have three identical foam dinos.

4. Remove the foam sheets' adhesive backing and stack the dinos on top of each other. Then stick the dinos to the glass.

5. Use the paintbrush to dab paint evenly onto the stack of foam dinos. Turn the glass over and press the dinosaurs onto the tote bag.

6. Continue applying paint and dabbing until the tote bag is decorated to your liking.

4.

5.

NOW TRY THIS!

To give your dinos an even, clean look, fill in the stamps with paint using a paintbrush.

Totally
TUBULAR

In sci-fi, experiments gone wrong often start out in test tubes. But this adorable chandelier couldn't be more right. Turn your room into a design lab with a bit of mad science!

What You'll Need:

24 plastic test tubes
with caps
small funnel
food coloring in
6 different colors
fishing line
12 inch (30.5 cm)
embroidery hoop

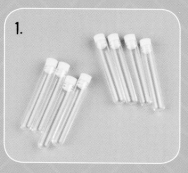

1.

Steps:

1. Divide the test tubes into groups of four.

2. Use the funnel to pour water into the first four test tubes. The tubes should be filled about 3/4 of the way.

3. Add food coloring one drop at a time to each test tube, until the water is the color you want. Push in the test tube's caps, and swirl gently. Use a different color of food coloring with each set of test tubes.

3.

NOW TRY THIS!

Create an ombre look by adding different amounts of food coloring to the test tubes. Start with a tiny amount in the first one. Then add a little more to each tube after.

 TURN THE PAGE

4. Wrap fishing line around the test tubes, just below the caps. Tie a double knot and cut off the short tail of the fishing line. Leave the other end of the fishing line long, so you can hang the tubes.

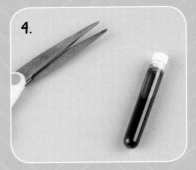

5. Repeat step 4, but wrap the line in the opposite direction. The knot should be on the other side of the tube.

6. Repeat steps 1-5 until all 24 tubes are filled.

7. To assemble the chandelier, separate the inside ring of the embroidery hoop from the outside ring.

8. Hang a test tube off the inside ring. Figure out how far down you want the tube to hang. Then wrap one piece of line around the hoop twice before tying it on. Repeat with the second line.

9. Continue tying the tubes to the hoop. The tubes should be about 2 inches (5 cm) apart. Hang the test tubes in a rainbow pattern, or alternate the colors.

10. When all the tubes are attached, re-assemble the embroidery hoop. The outer hoop will help keep the fishing wire in place.

11. Tie four pieces of fishing line an equal distance apart around the embroidery hoop. Tie the other ends together. Use the line to hang your chandelier.

NOW TRY THIS!

Don't have 24 test tubes? Use just a handful to make a suncatcher. Weave fishing wire between the tubes to wrap them together like panpipes. Or use the regular hanging instructions but attach them to something smaller, such as a macramé ring, a tool, a thick pen, or an old fork or spoon.

Blast-Off BOT

Why can't sci-fi robots be made with a piece of the past? Upcycle your bot to create an outdoor display of the future.

What You'll Need:

empty tin cans
sandpaper
old book pages
ribbon
washi tape
clear packing paper

recycled metal objects, such
    as hardware, magnets,
    scrubbies, silverware and
    utensils, and magnets
hot glue and hot glue gun (or
    industrial-strength glue)
hammer and nails
metal wire

Steps:

1. Rinse cans under hot water to remove any labels.
    Have an adult help you sand down any rough edges.

2. Mix and match different sized cans to make robots.
    You can make a robot out of one can, or stack two or
    three cans together for a large robot.

3. Use old book pages, ribbon, and washi tape to
    decorate the outside of the robot. Then cover
    everything with a layer of clear packing tape. This
    will protect the paper from rain and the outdoors.

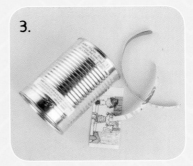

4. Decorate your robot with the recycled metal objects.
    Use hot glue—or industrial-strength glue, if you have
    an adult's help—to attach them. Get creative! Use old
    silverware and utensils for arms and legs. Magnets
    and recycled hardware, such as screws, washers,
    and bolts, can be used for facial features. Thin
    wires and springs make great hair!

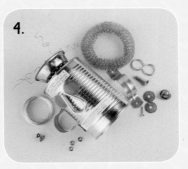

5. Have an adult help you hammer two holes near
    the top of the can.

6. Thread wire through the holes and bend or tie the
    ends. Use the wire to hang the robot.

NOW TRY THIS!

Wrap metal items with wire. This can give smooth
objects a different color or texture. You can also
use the wire to hang objects from your robot.

17

GROW-BOT

What happens to robots after all the humans are gone?
They collect soil and start growing new life! Give your
plants a sci-fi twist with these terra bots.

What You'll Need:

empty tin cans
hammer and nail
spray paint
recycled metal objects, such as hardware,
    magnets, scrubbies, silverware and
    utensils, and magnets
hot glue and hot glue gun, or
    industrial-strength glue
hammer and nails
metal wire
plant

Steps:

1. Fill the tin cans with water. Then put them in the freezer.

2. Once the water has frozen, remove the cans from the freezer. Have an adult help you use nails to hammer four holes in the bottom of each can.

3. Set the cans in a sink to let the water thaw and drain out. Wash and dry the cans, and remove any labels that might be stuck to them.

4. Set a dry can on a newspaper-covered workspace. Have an adult spray paint the outside of the can. Let the paint dry.

5. Use the recycled metal objects to decorate the Grow-Bot in a similar manner as the Blast-Off Bot. These bots will be sitting on the ground, so you can attach heavier items for arms and legs. Pair small cans with larger cans to make heads or body parts.

6. When your bot is ready, just add plants!

NOW TRY THIS!

Straws, brushes, and pushpins are other outdoor-safe items to use. Add bells for a little jingle! Other objects you could use include buttons, coils, bottle lids, soda tabs, drawer handles, and paper for decoration.

OFFBEAT OASIS

Imagine what life might be like on other planets by creating your own! Make an alien oasis for these cute creatures.

What You'll Need:

rocks
acrylic paint and paintbrushes
hot glue and hot glue gun
googly eyes
fine-tip paintbrush, permanent
    marker, or toothpick
medium-grit sandpaper
old metal tin, lunchbox, or other
    water-safe container
dirt
small cactus or succulent
sand
zip-top sandwich bag
food coloring

2.

Steps:

1. Wash off rocks, if necessary. Let them
   dry completely.

2. Paint the rocks. They can be solid colors, or you
   can add alienlike details like scales or textured
   dots. Let the paint dry completely.

3. Use hot glue to attach googly eyes to each rock.

4. Use a fine-tip paintbrush, permanent marker, or
   toothpick to give your aliens a mouth. Use white
   paint to make teeth pop.

5. To make your desert, remove the lid to your
   container. Add a layer of soil to the bottom of the
   tin. Place the cactus or succulent where you want
   it, and add a little more soil to support its roots.

7. Pour sand into a zip-top sandwich bag.
   Add a few drops of food coloring.

8. Shake the closed bag to get an even coat of
   colored sand.

9. Pour the colored sand on top of the soil. It should
   completely cover any dirt or plant roots.

10. Add your aliens!

7.

8.

SPACE CASE

The wonders of space have always had a special place in the sci-fi universe. Show off our solar system with this beaded bracelet.

What You'll Need:

polymer clay in a variety
of colors
small eye pins
polymer glaze
acrylic roller
craft knife
charm bracelet
two sets of jewelry pliers
jump rings

To Make Earth:

1. Pinch off a small amount of blue clay. Roll it around in your hands until it feels soft and pliable. Repeat with a small amount of green clay.

2. Stack the blue and green clay on top of each other. Then pinch together a little before rolling the clay into a ball.

3. Insert an eye pin into the top of the bead.

4. With an adult's help, follow the instructions on the clay's package to bake.

5. Once the clay is baked and cooled, add a coat of polymer glaze.

2.

3.

5.

NOW TRY THIS!

Use this technique to make the other rocky planets and moons.

TURN THE PAGE

To Make Jupiter:

1. Pinch off several small pieces of white, orange, red, brown, and yellow clay. Roll each piece in your hands until it feels soft and pliable.

2. Use the acrylic roller to flatten each piece into a very thin sheet. You should have 10 to 12 sheets of clay.

3. Layer each sheet on top of each other. Alternate the colors. Make sure the top and bottom sheets are the main color you want. Once they are stacked, use the acrylic roller to press them together.

4. Use the craft knife to cut the stack in half. Continue halving the stacks until they are around the bead size you want.

5. Carefully shape one of the stacks into a ball.

6. Insert an eye pin into the top of the bead.

7. With an adult's help, follow the instructions on the clay's package to bake.

8. Once the clay is baked and cooled, add a coat of polymer glaze.

NOW TRY THIS!

Use this technique to make other striped gas giant planets.

NOW TRY THIS!

To make Saturn, follow the instructions for Jupiter, but with light yellow, gold, and gray clay. To make Saturn's rings, cut and roll a thin strip of white clay. Wrap it around the planet, and trim off any excess.

1.

2.
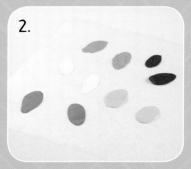

3.

4.

5.

To Make the Rest of the Planets:

1. Follow the instructions to make Earth, but use the suggested colors in the chart below.

Color Your Universe

Wondering what colors of clay to use? Use this handy color chart as inspiration for your planets.

Venus: gold, white, and brown

Mercury: gray and white

Mars: red, orange, and brown

Earth: blue and green

Jupiter: white, orange, red, brown, and yellow

Saturn: light yellow, gold, and grey

Uranus: blue, light blue, and white

Neptune: bright blue and purple

TURN THE PAGE

To Assemble Your Bracelet:

1. Lay each bead out in the proper order. Decide how you want them to be spaced on the bracelet.

2. Use the pliers to hold a jump ring steady while you work. Use the second set of pliers to pull the ring open.

3. Take one of the planet charms and thread it onto the jump ring.

4. Slide the open jump ring through the chosen link on your charm bracelet. Use pliers to close the jump ring securely.

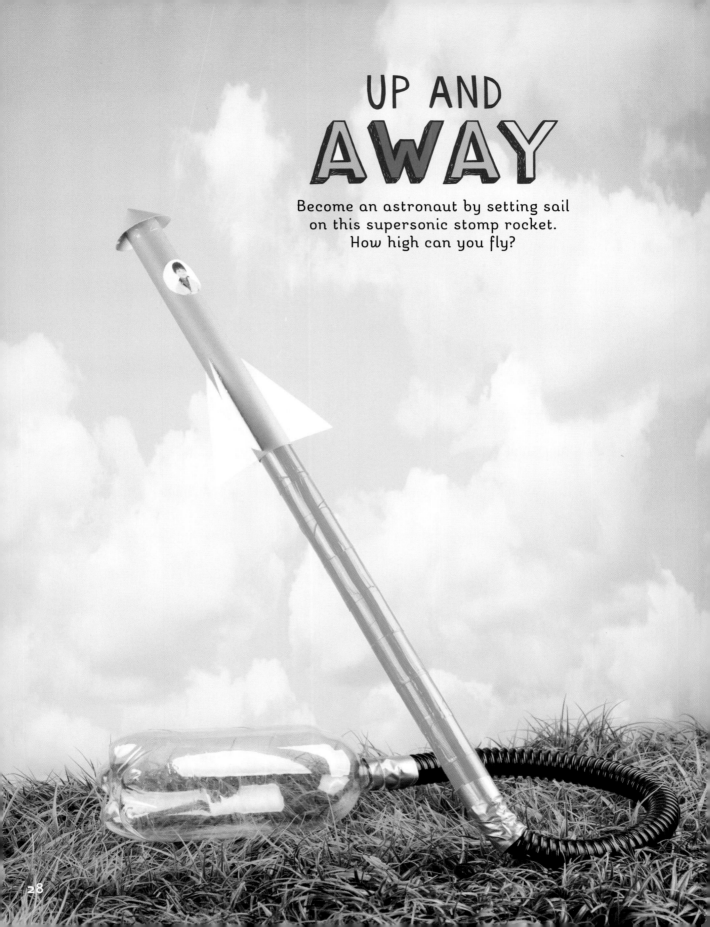

UP AND
AWAY

Become an astronaut by setting sail
on this supersonic stomp rocket.
How high can you fly?

What You'll Need:

several pieces of
    8 1/2-by-11-inch
    (21.6-by-28-cm)
    cardstock
2-foot (61-cm)-long piece
    of 1-inch (2.5-cm)
    PVC tube
clear tape
washi tape
hot glue and hot glue gun
empty 2 liter (67.6 fluid
    ounce) soda bottle
2-foot-long piece of
    1-inch vacuum hose
    or bike tube
duct tape
milk bottle lid
photograph of yourself

Steps:

1. Tightly wrap a piece of cardstock around the PVC tube. Tape the edges well. Then slide the cardstock off the tube.

2. Decorate the tube with washi tape.

3. Measure and cut a 2-inch (5-cm) wide circle out of the cardstock. Cut out a slice from about 1/6 of the circle. Then join the cut edges to make a cone shape, and tape together.

4. Use a little glue to attach the cone to the tube.

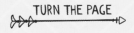

TURN THE PAGE

5. Place the milk bottle lid over your photograph. Trace around it, and then cut out the circle.

6. Glue the picture to the outside of the tube.

7. Cut out two 3-inch (7.6-cm)-tall triangles from the cardstock. Cut the triangles in half vertically. Glue them near the bottom of the cardstock tube.

8. Remove the soda bottle lid. Attach the hose to the bottle, and seal with duct tape.

9. Tape the PVC pipe to the other end of the hose.

10. To launch your rocket, set the soda bottle on the ground.

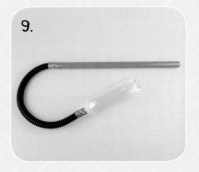

11. Have someone hold the PVC pipe straight up. Then slide the rocket onto the pipe.

12. Stomp on the bottle. Your rocket will shoot straight up in the air!

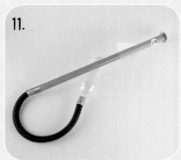